Michael Staack
China's Self-Conception and the
Security Environment in East Asia

WIFIS-aktuell
Book Series

Edited by

WIFIS – Academic Forum for International
Security, represented by

Prof. Dr. Johannes Varwick, Martin Luther
University Halle-Wittenberg

Volume 80

Michael Staack

China's Self-Conception and the Security Environment in East Asia

Is There (Still) a Chance
for Cooperative Security?

Verlag Barbara Budrich
Opladen • Berlin • Toronto 2025

A CIP catalogue record for this book is available from
Die Deutsche Nationalbibliothek (The German National Library):
https://portal.dnb.de.

© 2025   by Verlag Barbara Budrich GmbH, Opladen, Berlin & Toronto

ISBN   978-3-8474-3125-1 (Paperback)
eISBN   978-3-8474-3260-9 (PDF)
DOI   10.3224/84743125

Verlag Barbara Budrich GmbH
Stauffenbergstr. 7. D-51379 Leverkusen Opladen, Germany | info@budrich.de |
www.budrich.de

86 Delma Drive. Toronto, ON M8W 4P6 Canada | info@budrich.de | www.budrich.eu

Cover design by Walburga Fichtner, Köln, Germany
Typesetting by Angelika Schulz, Zülpich, Germany

Table of Contents

1 Preliminary Remarks

China's rise to become a global actor is a central development of international politics and will shape also the coming decades of the 21st century. How to deal with this rising world power is an issue of an increasingly controversial debate; in science, politics and the media. In this debate, analyses and opinions are driven by various – rather contradictory and in part mutually exclusive – motives: the challenging shaping of the further integration into a functioning international order of a global political actor that is gaining in power; the reform of this order and its adaptation to framework conditions that will continue to change; the maintenance of a globalised economic system that is based on the division of labour; the handling of planetary challenges such as climate change, pandemics and arms control, which can only be dealt with transnationally; the assertion of democracy against apparently or actually capable autocratic alternatives; the containment of distribution conflicts and social divisions in the western industrialised countries in view of the continued economic rise of China and other Asian states; the maintenance of the primacy of the United States and the dominance of the West in the international system; the consideration of the interests and demands of the Global South through real politics instead of rhetoric – and, not least, the self-assertion of the European Union (EU).

The EU, with its threefold approach comprising competition, partnership and systemic rivalry with the People's Republic of China, has established a strategy since 2019 that is essentially intelligent and sustainable. The German Federal Government adopted a similar approach with its *China Strategy*. Of course, the order of these three components may change – mainly depending on China's actions but also on other framework conditions. What is decisive is the continued adherence to the threefold approach. A particular challenge lies in explicitly defining the tension between the contradictory concepts of cooperation and rivalry – up to and including confrontation. Experience from the East-West conflict has shown that an *antagonistic cooperation* that incorporates these concepts is possible. Unfortunately, this experience has to a large extent disappeared from the active institutional memory of political administrations. However, it can be reactivated and used for a strategic policy which, unlike that of the East-West conflict, also has to consider completely different influencing factors such as the progressive shifts in economic and political power in the international system. An approach that includes both cooperation in certain areas and deliberate rivalry in others is now more necessary than ever as the handling of planetary challenges cannot wait – and will not succeed by adhering to the maxim that the West can solve the world's problems. This era is over.

One of the reasons why the EU and Germany are well-advised to hold on to their own strategy and position on the People's Republic of China is that they have interests of their own. The changed framework conditions of recent years include the fact that the policy (and reliability) of the United States, at present and for the foreseeable future, is only calculable for the respective electoral period of four years. The very good cooperation between the Biden administration and the EU member states in view of the brutal war of aggression that Russia is waging against Ukraine in violation of international law cannot conceal the fact that the division within the United States has deepened further and that the Republican Party is dominated by Donald Trump and like-minded people. With such forces, a common world policy based on democratic values and international cooperation will hardly be possible, unless the EU wanted to seriously damage its reputation. It would also be short-sighted and run counter to increasing the Union's freedom of action and "strategic autonomy" to compensate for the necessary reduction of dependencies on other countries, for example Russia and China, by increasing existing dependencies on the United States. Although it seems highly unlikely at the moment that the structural division of the United States will be overcome, this objective is of course in the interest of its European allies.

There is no doubt that the policy of the People's Republic of China has changed considerably under its head of state and party leader Xi Jinping. Re-ideologisation, control and the rollback of domestic pluralism; the extensive elimination of Hong Kong's self-administration; repression including serious human rights violations in Xinjiang province; military demonstrations of power directed at Taiwan and, in general, an end to its rather cautious policy in favour of boastful world power ambitions have become a reality. However, it must not be ignored that China's successful rise has mobilised counter-forces which seek to deny such a rise to any ascending power on principle. This, too, generates tensions and demonstrates an ahistorical worldview. No hegemony exists forever. In addition, there are complicated unresolved issues from World War II due to the fact that no peace settlements exist in East Asia.

The wisdom and sustainability of the policy represented by Xi Jinping must be strongly doubted. At best, its track record is ambivalent. One-man rule and long terms of office almost inevitably have negative effects; the latter also applies to democracies. Subject-specific opposition and, as appropriate, steadfastness in relations with Xi's China remain necessary. It must be ensured, however, that the opportunities for the required cooperation with China remain intact. The following general observation also remains correct: China's current policy is not an end stage of history; the future remains open – and can be influenced from outside, especially through dialogue and connections.

The Russian war of aggression against Ukraine, which began on 24 February 2022, represents a turning point for European security, but it also has far-reaching implications for the international order and the wider Indo-Pacific region. The Chinese leadership hovers between the fundamental condemnation of the war, blaming the United States and NATO with regard to the causes of the conflict, maintaining its close strategic partnership with Russia, and its efforts to not further strain the relations in the Indo-Pacific region and with the EU. In general, the People's Republic of China respects Western sanctions against Russia despite the fact that those sanctions are not applied within the United Nations framework. Beijing recognises neither the annexation of Ukrainian territories (2022) by Moscow nor the annexation of Crimea (2014). President Putin's nuclear threats are being criticised. Based on its cost-benefit calculation, the People's Republic of China is currently not prepared to act as a mediator. This may change. China continues to have a fundamental interest in a stable international environment for its economic development.

This text was first presented in the autumn of 2020 as a discussion paper for the Study Group on European Security and Peace of the Association of German Scientists (https://vdw-ev.de/ueber-uns/studiengruppen/europ-sicher heit-frieden) and has since been revised and updated several times. I am extremely grateful to my colleagues in the study group for their comments, in particular their criticism and suggestions, and I would also like to thank my peers in international relations, peace and conflict research, Sinology and East Asian studies. For this version in English (completed on 22 August 2024), the originally chosen presentation of pointed theses and the limited use of footnotes have been retained. The text and the selection of additional literature are intended to encourage a more intensive study of topics that will remain on the agenda in the foreseeable future: China's self-conception, the conflict constellations in the Indo-Pacific, the Sino-American competition and the options for action of the EU and Germany in the areas of cooperation, conflict and conflict management and peacekeeping.

2   China's Self-Conception

1. China's economic, technological, political, military and scientific rise is one of the most important developments in recent history. In terms of speed and multidimensionality, it is historically unprecedented. The People's Republic itself regards this development as *a comeback*; a return to a leading global position which the country had occupied in eighteen of twenty centuries AD and was destroyed by the interventions of the imperialist powers in the long "Century of Humiliation" (1840–1949). The rise of China has a significant impact both on the international system and on the regional constellations in East Asia and the wider Indo-Pacific region.[1] There is little evidence that this process, which has been unfolding since the beginning of the reform and opening-up policy in 1978, can be stopped or even reversed; however, it can be slowed down by wrong domestic policy decisions and by the actions of external actors.[2] It will be decisive which concepts and strategies China itself and the international environment – in this order – will apply to deal with this rise in the future.

   The probable rise of China to become the largest economy in the world, which could take place in the 2030s, would constitute another global turning point. Economic power shifts carrying political and economic consequences could intensify even further. A market of this size can only be "decoupled" to a very limited extent. However, in view of the general volatility of international politics, the economic consequences of Russia's war of aggression against Ukraine and the US embargoes and sanctions against China –especially with regard to high technology, forecasts on

---

1   "Indo-Pacific" is not a region but a political concept. The United States, India, Australia, Japan, as well as France and Germany, have different understandings of this concept. The concept of comprehensive securitisation and containment of China was initially only supported by the United States and Japan, whereas Germany, in its policy guidelines for the Indo-Pacific (2020), advocates an inclusive approach that also includes the People's Republic. In political science, it is East Asia, South Asia and South East Asia that tend to be considered as political, socially constructed and overlapping regions.

2   In addition, by „unknown unknowns" or "black swans" such as unforeseeable disasters; for example, a war in East Asia.

medium-term developments –must be assessed with caution. For China, there is no automatism to become the "Number One Economy".

2. Today, China regards itself as a global policy-shaper, an economic power, a major power in Asia and as the largest developing country in the world – a "country developing itself" would probably be more appropriate. As a power of discourse, it wants to influence the development of the rules, norms and institutions of the international system and actively contribute to shaping the global agenda. To this end, China develops its own narratives which refer to China's success story of the past decades. These narratives are intended to establish Chinese concepts and norms in a changing international order.

China's rise, by and large, took place within the framework of the existing international order, in particular the security and economic order. China wants to make changes to this order and/or sectoral partial orders according to its own ideas, but not overthrow them. While this objective is legitimate, it requires the formation of international majorities or consensus. China underestimates the extent to which the present system and its subsystems are rooted in Western norms. The dominant Western discourse usually ignores the fact that the hegemony of the United States and its understanding of world order are not enshrined in the Charter of the United Nations and nor is the concept of the United States as a guardian of the *global commons* that is above the rules-based order.

China's external relations can best be characterised as *policy of connectivity* (cf. Godehardt 2020). The country is striving to create a global mesh of economic cooperation through networks and structures which is also intended to lead to an increased politico-diplomatic weight in the world. The most important objective of China's foreign policy is to maximise prosperity and to ensure the favourable conditions required for this.

3. From the point of view of the People's Republic, the international order is determined by the *primacy* of the United States and its allies. The Chinese demand for a democratisation of international relations is aimed at replacing this hegemony with a multipolar and multilateral system. China does not want to replace the United States as the world's leading power but to be recognised as an actor equal to the United States in all policy areas in such a multipolar system – at least until the middle of the 21st century. It cannot achieve greater ambitions as the country lacks important power resources such as alliance systems which it traditionally rejects. From the Chinese point of view, states are still the decisive actors in the international system.

4. China's foreign policy is defined by its own traditions of thinking, but also very much by neo-realistic influences. While constructivist or liberal perspectives of theories of international relations are known, in science and politics they are mostly regarded as less relevant or not structure-determining. Even though rhetorically other priorities are often set, China's understanding and performance of its role as a global great power are based on its perception of the United States' foreign policy behaviour; as evidenced, for example, by the selective non-compliance with international law, a strong military, military or economic power projection, the rejection of compulsory arbitration or the demand for "respect". The ideology of "socialism with Chinese face" is only of limited relevance to the country's foreign policy.

   With regard to certain core interests (global influence, the *nine-dash line*, non-negotiable territorial integrity of China including Hong Kong, Taiwan, Tibet, Xinjiang), a democratic China would most likely not differ significantly from today's autocratic China when it comes to foreign policy.

5. China pursues its interests both by using the robust means of traditional great power politics and as a *responsible stakeholder* in the international system. With regard to *global governance*, it holds on to multilateralism and tries to enforce its interests within this framework. Correspondingly, China prefers bilateral patterns of relations, within the framework of which it can fully exploit its economic strength. The successive Chinese (2016) and German (2017) presidencies of the Group of Twenty (G20) – the content of which had been closely coordinated – were productive in terms of results and were also assessed as positive by the Federal Government of Germany. China is staying away from the Western Group of Seven (G7) because it does not, as a matter of principle, join cooperations in which it cannot play an active shaping role. Even though *global governance* remains necessary and even irreplaceable for its content, this concept has come under criticism due to the double effect of the US concepts of *decoupling* and *containment* and due to the calling into question of the economic globalisation process so far (not only) as a result of the COVID–19 pandemic and the Russian war of aggression. The abandonment or downgrading of *global governance* would weaken an important strategy for the (self-)integration of China into an inclusive world order policy.

6. China's national economy influences, changes and shapes the international economic relations by its size alone. If the country, politically desired, pursues innovations in certain industrial or technological fields, this has

direct impacts up to displacement effects or the assumption of market leadership on a global scale.

For more than 100 states, including Germany, the People's Republic has become the most important trading partner. This development has led to dependencies on the Chinese market (e.g., for the German automotive industry). Nevertheless, interdependencies prevail, because China's economy has also become dependent on the growth of foreign trade and access to markets and has integrated itself into global supply chains. The new Chinese strategy of *dual circulation* pursued since 2020 – developed in response to the US embargo and sanctions policy and aimed at sustainably strengthening the internal market – will only take effect in the medium-term.

Based on China's specialisation advantages, such as market size, extremely high growth and profit margins for a long time, Chinese companies have exploited the WTO rules and the requirement to establish *joint ventures* and used them for unilateral advantages, rule violations, industrial espionage and theft of intellectual property. At the same time, China has implemented the WTO dispute settlement body's rulings issued against it. To be sure, China's economic rise was accelerated by the violation of rules. However, the practices China uses are not exceptional. From a comparative historical perspective, they are in line with the policies of other ascending economic powers, e.g., the United States and the German Empire before 1914. With the increasing economic and technological success of these states, the use of such practices decreased significantly – a development that may also be expected with respect to China. This could promote the *reciprocity* with respect to market access and framework conditions that the EU rightly demands. The extent to which *decoupling* and embargo policies advanced by the United States influence this development cannot be estimated at present.

7. Under the leadership of the head of state and party leader Xi Jinping, who has been in office since 2012, the country's policy has changed significantly. Until 2049, the 100th anniversary of the founding of the People's Republic of China, the large-scale comeback as a world power is to be completed, and, according to China's own claim, it is to be characterised by economic, technological and military strength, sustainable and innovative action, domestic stability and cultural appeal. At home, Xi Jinping relies on re-ideologisation, disciplining and control, especially in the digital sphere, in order to curb domestic pluralism and consolidate the rule of the party in power. His campaign against corruption, which remains very popular, also serves this objective. In Xinjiang province, China's political leaders have established an extremely repressive regime that violates

fundamental human rights of large parts of the Uyghur ethnic group; in the Hong Kong Special Administrative Region, fundamental rights and political participation are drastically restricted. Other turning points are the abandoning of the collective leadership principle pursued since 1978, the enabling of a potentially lifelong term in office of the head of state and party leader, and the inclusion of his "thoughts" in the constitution and the party statutes.

It is most likely that the assumption of office by Xi Jinping and his markedly changed policy constitute the biggest turning point since the beginning of the Chinese economic reform, also known as reform and opening-up. Until Xi's assumption of office, a precarious tense relationship existed between economic liberalisation and political liberalisation. China has never been on the road to becoming a Western democracy. However, there had been progress with respect to fundamental freedoms and the rule of law. This development seems to have come to an end. It remains at least questionable whether the success story of China's rise can be continued under the conditions of re-ideologisation, disciplining and control.

8. The political system of the People's Republic of China is incompatible with Western concepts of democracy and rule of law. While this observation has been true for the last seven decades, in recent years, it has not only become more apt again but the situation has become even more serious. The development of a state based on the rule of law with an independent judiciary, which in Western countries paved the way for democracy, is currently out of the question. Also, a common understanding of universal human rights, in particular the classical civil liberties and rights to participation, does not seem either possible in the foreseeable future. Within the United Nations, China, thanks to its expedient policy, is by no means isolated. With regard to both Xinjiang and Hong Kong, more states support China's line of action than the Western criticism against it, while the majority of states refrain from taking a stance. However, it still makes sense to engage in dialogues on human rights and the rule of law with China; even if just to put controversial issues on the agenda again and again.

China's line of action in Xinjiang and Hong Kong can be attributed to various motives, primarily to a technocratic authoritarian understanding of politics based on *peace and order*. At the same time, it reflects the People's Republic leaders' perception of Western politics: in its calculation of interests, the Chinese government obviously does not expect the West to make any concessions in return for its own concessions and has therefore opted for a policy of repression.

Obviously, China is not the only country in the world with an autocratic model. Depending on the criteria, the list of autocratic states comprises 30 to 40 percent or even more out of all states, among them many close partners of the West such as Saudi Arabia, the United Arab Emirates and NATO member Turkey. China's autocratic model has only become a perceived challenge for the West because of its relative success and the country's power resources.

3 Conflicts: South China Sea and Taiwan

1. In its legally binding ruling on the dispute between the Philippines and China handed down on 12 July 2016, the International Court of Arbitration rejected the Chinese claims regarding the maritime area disputed between the two states. However, already in 2006, China excluded maritime territorial disputes from its ratification of compulsory arbitration, did not participate in the proceedings and announced that it would not accept the arbitral ruling. The Chinese position – the *nine-dash line* – had already been defined by the Republic of China in 1947/49 and is still upheld, also by Taiwan.

   The dispute over territorial rights in the South China Sea is a legally and politically extremely complex conflict that is difficult to settle, since: (a) it is an international order issue involving a dispute over the applicability and interpretation of the United Nations Convention on the Law of the Sea (UNCLOS), (b) it concerns disputes between China and various of its neighbouring states, and hence a regional problem, (c) the dispute is part of the Sino-American competition for power, had been increasingly politically and militarily charged since 2016, and had for a certain period become the decisive symbolic conflict over the capability to exert hegemony in the Indo-Pacific region (before it was replaced by the conflict over Taiwan in 2022).

   The matter in dispute must also be given a multidimensional consideration: (a) it is about the enforcement of sovereignty, (b) likewise, it is also about access to resources, in particular to oil, gas and fishing grounds, (c) security policy and military strategy are also of relevance, i.e., the extension of the People's Liberation Army's options afforded by the secure access to the high seas.

   The different positions the states are taking in this conflict have existed for more than 70 years and thus, partly date back to the colonial era. The charging of the conflict in recent years can mainly be explained by power shifts towards China, China's fait accompli policy (i.e., as implemented by the building of artificial islands) and the increasing Sino-American competition.

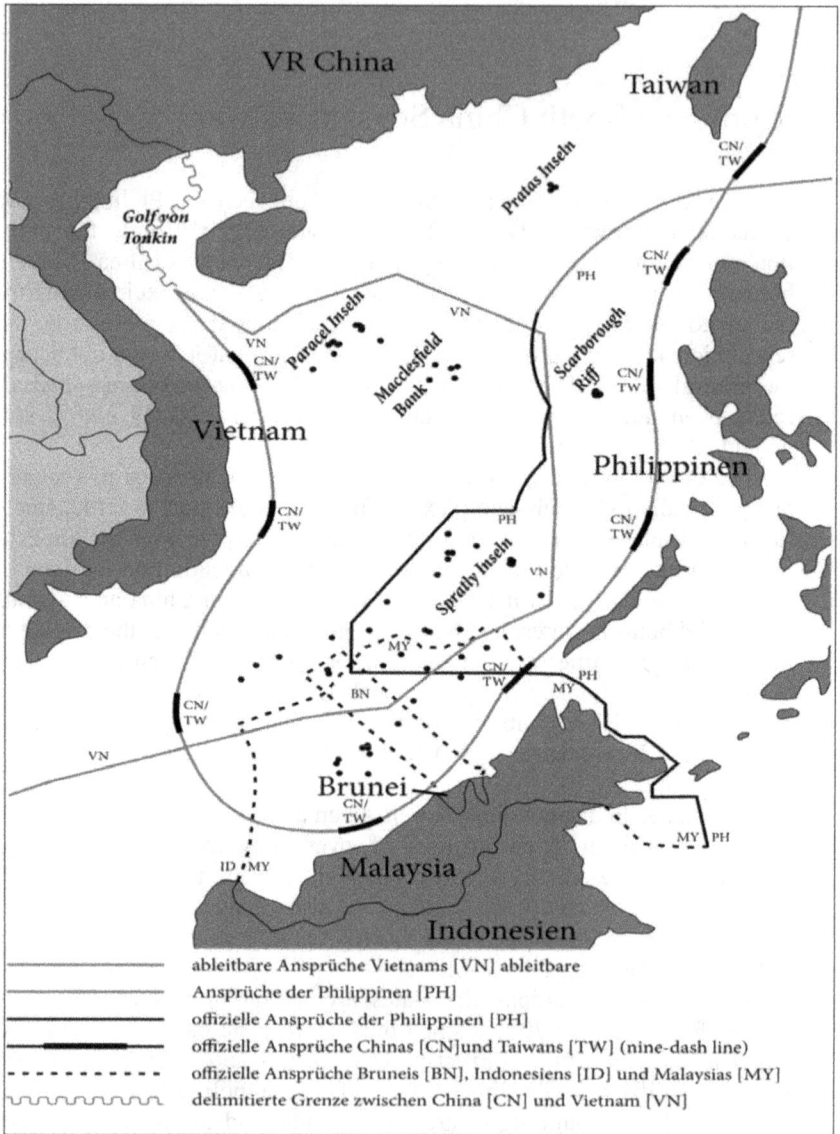

Figure 1: Official and derivable territorial and maritime claims in the South China Sea. Source: Kreuzer 2014.

Glossary

VR China	People's Republic of China
Taiwan	Taiwan
Golf von Tonkin	Gulf of Tonkin
Pratas Inseln	Pratas Islands
Paracel Inseln	Paracel Islands
Vietnam	Vietnam
Philippinen	Philippines
Spratly Inseln	Spratly Islands
Brunei	Brunei
Malaysia	Malaysia
Indonesien	Indonesia
ableitbare Ansprüche Vietnams [VN]	derivable claims of Vietnam [VN]
ableitbare Ansprüche der Philippinen [PH]	derivable claims of the Philippines [PH]
offizielle Ansprüche der Philippinen [PH]	official claims of the Philippines [PH]
offizielle Ansprüche Chinas [CN] und Taiwans [TW] (nine-dash line)	official claims of China [CN] and Taiwan [TW] (nine-dash line)
offizielle Ansprüche Bruneis [BN], Indonesiens [ID] und Malaysias [MY]	official claims of Brunei [BN], Indonesia [ID] and Malaysia [MY]
delimitierte Grenze zwischen China [CN] und Vietnam [VN]	delimited border between China [CN] and Vietnam [UN]

This example shows once again that compulsory arbitration is only a suitable instrument for resolving conflicts if a convergence of positions has already been initiated and if the parties to the conflict are prepared to accept the arbitral award in the first place. The United States has not joined the UNCLOS and only recognises the Convention with reservations. As a matter of principle, the United States rejects compulsory arbitration. In its National Security Strategy of 1996 (Clinton II), the United States argued that while UNCLOS restricted the freedom of action of other states to the benefit of the United States, Washington's accession was not desirable as it would restrict its own military options. France (1996) and Great Britain (2003) have expressed similar reservations to those of China. So, the three Western leading powers want to force China to meet standards that they do not comply with themselves.[3]

2. In addition to the territorial conflicts in the South China Sea, the multi-dimensional conflict over Taiwan has also become increasingly politically and military charged. As a result of this process, this decades-long restricted conflict could become the cause of a military escalation with

---

3   Germany has both recognized the compulsory arbitration within the scope of UNCLOS and the arbitral award of 2016. The EU member states failed to reach a common position, among other things, because Croatia does not accept a ruling given by the International Court of Arbitration on a dispute with Slovenia.

global consequences, possibly even resulting in a confrontation similar to the *Cuban Missile Crisis* of 1962. Reducing tensions in and around Taiwan and reaching an agreement on a workable *modus vivendi* are at present probably the most important foreign policy tasks for China and the United States in their bilateral relations. Currently, however, both sides are engaged in an action-reaction process in which quest for prestige and shows of force dominate on both sides.

3. The main causes for the charging of the conflict are four interrelated circumstances: (a) ambiguities or different understandings of the *One China policy* by the People's Republic of China, the United States and the Republic of Taiwan, (b) unilateral deviations from the current status quo by the United States and the People's Republic, (c) the clear will of the majority of Taiwan's population for independence and thus, the rejection of a unification with the People's Republic of China and, as always when considering the security constellation in East Asia, (d) Beijing's comprehensive increase in power. Backed by the growth in its economic, military and political power resources, China, by making threatening gestures, makes it unmistakably clear that it will not accept anything that it considers to be deviations from the status quo.

    Therefore, the conflict over Taiwan comprises several dimensions: (a) it is a conflict about the territorial affiliation of the island, (b) by now, it has also become a conflict about values, the contrast between the communist autocracy in Beijing and the meanwhile established pluralistic democracy in Taiwan, which a part of the West regards as an alternative model for a democratic China, (c) above all, it is also a prestige conflict between the People's Republic and the United States over the regional hegemony in East Asia and, in addition and on a larger scale, the competition for power and systemic and military supremacy. Furthermore, (d) there is an economic and technological dimension as Taiwanese companies have developed into world leaders in the microelectronics industry and especially in semiconductor production. The belief that the Taiwan conflict would solve itself over time, which was still the guiding principle in the 1970s and was upheld until the beginning of this century, is definitely a thing of the past.

4. Until 1895, Taiwan was a province of the Chinese Empire. It had to be ceded to Japan as a result of the First Sino-Japanese War (1894–95) and was returned to China in 1945. After the Communist Party's victory in the Chinese civil war, the defeated Kuomintang (KMT) government under marshal Chiang Kai-shek fled to the island, where it established a military dictatorship that lasted until 1987. Both the People's Republic of China

and the Republic of China in Taiwan claimed to be the legitimate representative of the whole of China. Until 1971, the military regime represented China in the United Nations and held the permanent seat on the UN Security Council. In the course of the rapprochement between the United States and the People's Republic of China in the early 1970s, the UN General Assembly recognised the mainland's communist government as the only legitimate representative of China and

"decides to restore all its rights to the People's Republic of China and to recognize the representatives of its Government as the only legitimate representatives of China to the United Nations, and to expel forthwith the representatives of Chiang Kai-shek from the place which they unlawfully occupy at the United Nations and in all the organizations related to it" (United Nations 1971).

The United States, too, broke off its diplomatic relations with the Republic of China, terminated the bilateral treaty of alliance and established diplomatic relations with the People's Republic in 1978. As early as 1972, the United States, in the Joint Communiqué of the United States of America and the People's Republic of China on the future relations, had acknowledged that there is but one China:

"The U.S. side declared: The United States acknowledges that all Chinese on either side of the Taiwan Strait maintain there is but one China and that Taiwan is a part of China. The United States Government does not challenge that position" (United States Department of State Office of the Historian 1972).

The United States did not object to the reunification of China, but insisted on a peaceful process. In the early 1970s, the Nixon administration (1969–74) assumed that such a reunification would take place in the foreseeable future. This attitude met with considerable resistance in the United States Congress that enacted the Taiwan Relations Act in 1979. This act intended the continuation of bilateral relations below the level of diplomatic recognition, but above all guaranteed the military dictatorship arms deliveries in order to ensure its defence capability. The government in Beijing regarded this as a violation of the Joint Communiqué of 1972, yet it adhered to its expectation that a reunification would take place. With the democratisation of Taiwan after 1987, the end of the hitherto unbroken rule by the KMT and increasing efforts to achieve statehood, the framework conditions changed fundamentally. Nevertheless, the early 1990s saw the successful institutionalisation of economic and political ties between China and Taiwan and brought about a wide range of predominantly commercial exchanges.

5. As early as 2005, the People's Republic of China made it clear by passing the Anti-Secession Law that it would respond militarily to a declaration of

independence by Taiwan. The unification with Taiwan is a prominent core interest of Beijing. The large-scale military exercises and other threating gestures follow exactly this logic and signal that China's determination should not be questioned. They also contribute to a further charging and potential escalation of the conflict. By largely abandoning the rule of law and self-administration in the Hong Kong Special Administrative Region (2019/20), the People's Republic discredited the previously propagated principle of "*One country, two systems*" and spurred efforts for national independence in Taiwan.

Starting with the Trump administration in 2017, the United States has somewhat distanced itself from its long-standing policy of *strategic ambiguity*. President Biden has declared three times since 2021 that he would provide military support to Taiwan in the event of a Chinese attack, without making the usual reservations (no declaration of independence by Taiwan).[4] Subsequently, his administration has invariably declared that the policy of strategic ambiguity had not changed. This opens the opportunity for a clarification by the United States through diplomatic channels. Leading Republican politicians of the *Make America Great Again* mainstream, such as former Secretary of State Mike Pompeo, demand the recognition of Taiwan's independence. Such a step would amount to a declaration of war. This is also clear to these politicians.

In the East Asia and the Indo-Pacific regions, the overwhelming majority of states are not interested in a war over Taiwan or in a Sino-American military conflict in general. That understanding constitutes a good starting point for common efforts for de-escalation to which the EU, ASEAN and other states can make their individual contributions.

---

4 Previous administrations – up to Barack Obama (2009–17) – had always been very clear in their statements in this respect. In 2003, President George W. Bush stated that the United States supported the One-China policy and rejected Taiwan's independence (cf. The White House 2003). For example, in 2007, his Secretary of State Condoleezza Rice declared: "We do not support independence for Taiwan. [...] We think that Taiwan's referendum to apply to the United Nations under the name 'Taiwan' is a provocative policy" (United States Department of State 2007).

4 The Perception of China in the World

1. In recent years, the view on China has again become strongly determined by stereotypes ("attacking dragon", "yellow peril", "economic rise without limits") – at least in Germany's mainstream media. This can be read as a counterstrategy to a more differentiated way of thinking. Since the basic knowledge about China and Asia is generally rather limited in comparison to the knowledge about the United States and Russia, stereotypes about China and Asia potentially have the strongest effect.

2. The rise of China leads to justified, understandable fears, uncertainties and defensive reactions in the West and in the region; to strategies of balancing, containment, decoupling and also rollback. China is perceived as a power that has a grand strategy, the economic power and financial resources to pursue it, and the willingness to enforce its interests also against resistance. In particular, the neo-realist *China Threat* school of thought attributes intentions to the People's Republic similar to those that are or have been pursued by present and former Western great powers themselves. The *Belt and Road Initiative* (BRI), in particular, is deemed a cipher for China's ambitions – the large and multifaceted project of a New Silk Road, which is intended to provide China with an enhanced and sustainable link mainly with Central Asia, Europe and Africa, and in which about 120 states participate to very different degrees of cooperation. The authoritarian Chinese way of governance is also perceived as a challenge for liberal democracy. China's ambivalent conduct during the COVID-19 pandemic has intensified these perceptions even more. In 2019/20, Beijing's suppression of the democracy movement in Hong Kong and its departure from the principle of "One country, two systems" marked another turning point.

3. As far as China's negative perception is concerned, five factors are usually overlooked: (a) The power shifts in the international system inevitably lead to a much stronger presence of Asia throughout the world. This applies in particular to the People's Republic of China. China is increasingly becoming what the United States and the members of the EU as a whole already are: a global, namely, also permanently globally visible actor. (b) China has strategies for its further economic and political rise. The implementation of these strategies, however, requires a

peaceful environment, partnerships and consideration for the interests of third parties. In projects such as the BRI, the military dimension plays only a limited role. (c) "China in the world" is not a uniform actor but a cipher for a variety of actors, such as the central government, provincial and municipal governments, private and state-owned companies, foundations – including Chinese small-scale merchants in almost every corner of Africa and other parts of the world. (d) As described, China's rise took place at an unprecedented speed. The *smartness* of China's conduct in the world has not kept pace with this, as exemplified by the counterproductive *Wolf Warrior diplomacy* of the years 2020/21. As regards the use of *soft power* resources and traditional, let alone astute diplomacy, China has a lot to catch up on. (e) China's ambitious projects involve many uncertainties and risks and the mastering of these cannot be taken for granted. Moreover, in recent years, China has been repeating Western policy mistakes and adding mistakes by its own. This may result in increased *self-containment*, as it was observed in 2020, when, at least in some parts of the world (such as the EU), China's boasting vaccine diplomacy achieved the opposite of what was intended.

4. With regard to China, too, the "end of history" is open. The rule and ideology of Xi Jinping will not determine the development of this dynamic and complex country in the long term. A return to limited pluralism, greater participation and openness are just as possible as the sclerotising establishment of a controlling autocracy, a successful output autocracy or disruptive breaks. The same applies to the country's role in world politics and its foreign policy. Autocracy and *restraint* in international politics can go hand in hand, as can, conversely, opening up and reform at the domestic level and aggressive nationalist behaviour at the international level.

Actors in the international system are well advised to perceive this openness of the future in order to be able to promote developments that are conducive to peace policy – as far as this is possible from the outside.

5 Regional Security and Sino-American Competition for Power, Systemic and Military Supremacy

1. An extensive competition for power and systemic and military supremacy has emerged between the USA and the People's Republic of China. At the core of the conflict lies the competition for power. The USA would not accept being caught up or overtaken even by a democratic China (as by a democratic Japan in the 1980s), just as it is not willing to recognise the democratic EU as an equal pole of power. The systemic competition fuels the competition for power further since the Western democratic model and China's authoritarian party-state model are indeed incompatible with each other. In this extensive competition, China's political system is its biggest weakness. This is the reason why China is not an attractive model for most of the world, regardless of its effectiveness. However, the Chinese development model with a strong state control is increasingly becoming more attractive due to the quickening succession of crises of Western capitalism that has been unleashed in a neo-liberal manner since the 1980s.

   Military competition is a function derived from competition for power and systemic supremacy, which to an extent can acquire a momentum of its own, but which – depending on the respective cost-benefit calculation – is generally open to containment or regulation, for example by arms control. This objective will be impossible to achieve by way of a comprehensive confrontation.

   The times of *bipartisanship* in US foreign policy have long been a thing of the past. With regard to its external relations, the USA is a deeply divided and polarised country. This does *not* apply to the opposition to China that is shared across parties or political camps, firmly anchored in Congress and thus, contributes to the country's identity and its effect on the global political self-image of the USA.

   At present, the United States will not be able to achieve long-term success in the competition for power and military supremacy against China and Russia at the same time – even with the full support of its allies (which is unlikely in this form). This is certainly true in military terms, but most probably also in economic and technological terms.[5] In this respect, the narrative of the *great power competition* between the big players USA, Russia and China, while has become reality, has not been logically thought through. China – with its large population and its economic, technological and innovative potential – and Russia – as the world's most resource-rich country and with the largest nuclear arsenal – complement each other very well. However, both are neither natural allies nor is their relationship symmetrical. China does not recognise the annexation of Crimea and other Ukrainian territories, and nor does Russia recognise China's territorial claims in the South China Sea.

Russia's war of aggression against Ukraine is incompatible with China's interest in a stable, peaceful environment for its economic development. The close cooperation between the two states over the past few years is mainly, though not exclusively, the result of Western politics or corresponding common interests resulting from it; supplemented by path dependencies, e.g., in armaments cooperation. It is in the interest of European and German politics not to address "China and Russia" as a bloc, but as two different actors whose interests coincide in part and conflict in part.

2. In East and South Asia, the system of states does not count on a comprehensive, functionally adequate, working and sufficiently institutionalised cooperation structure. Numerous territorial conflicts are still unresolved, there is a lack of effective security institutions, and the burdens of the past have only been dealt with insufficiently, if at all. In many countries, nationalism dominates. Above all, *empathy*, which is the basic prerequisite for any realistic, peace-promoting foreign and security policy, is missing on almost all sides. In short, East Asia but also South Asia are caught in an inadequately contained *security dilemma*, which the increasing degree of economic interdependencies so far has helped to mitigate to only a limited extent (*Asian paradox*).

---

5 The same is true for China. China and Russia, in turn, will most likely not be able to win the competition for systemic supremacy. While Russia is a classic autocracy, the People's Republic of China gains appeal due to its high degree of output legitimacy. However, it is doubtful whether this will be sufficient on a global scale if it is not complemented by participation and pluralism.

Six dimensions of analysis are important for understanding the political and economic developments in East and South Asia:

- the regional dynamics with their processes of cooperation, competition and conflict
- the Sino-American competition for power, which is in conflict with the regional dynamics and increasingly overlaps them
- the comparatively poor establishment of governance or institutionalisation and a state-centred understanding of politics
- the specifically Asian ways of dealing with conflicts (e.g., priority of process over result; saving of *face*)
- a history that is ridden with conflicts and that aggravates them
- the role of external actors.

3. China is not (yet) big enough to dominate the region, but it is too big to be considered as an *equal among equals*. China's economic rise leads to interdependencies and actual dependencies. At the global level, China's military modernisation will not pose a challenge to the US for a long time yet. In the East Asia region, however, it restricts the options of America which sees its hegemony threatened. In addition, the military build-up and modernisation process changes the balance of forces in the region, although Japan or South Korea (and, of course, the USA) still have a technological advantage over China. There is no agreed or recognised "standard" for an adequate strength of the People's Liberation Army. In its self-perception as a great power, China measures its potential against that of the USA, especially with regard to the navy and special forces. For most neighbours, China's military build-up, combined with its territorial claims and a general gain in power, seems threatening or destabilising. Ultimately, the security dilemma can only be sustainably contained through arms control – bi- and multilaterally, as well as sectorally with regard to conventional and nuclear systems or different ranges. On the one hand, at present, China does not consider itself to be in a sufficiently strong position yet to negotiate key arms control issues. On the other hand, the USA seeks to establish its superiority – arms control will not be possible on this basis either.

In the last years, China has started to modernize and enlarge its strategic nuclear weapons arsenal. The perceived security dilemma deriving from US containment strategies and a policy aiming at a higher potential for global leverage seemed to be guiding for that development. Nevertheless, the United States and the Russian Federation possess more than 90% of strategic nuclear weapons, and China is very far away from a comparable position. China has stated that its policies of *nuclear non-first use* and *minimum deterrence* will not change. Measures of transparency and an explanation of its doctrine might contribute to confidence-building especially towards the US. Such a policy would also strengthen China's position as a responsible nuclear power.

4. The new US strategy in the Pacific (*Pivot to Asia*) proclaimed in 2011 – that is, before Xi Jinping took office – did not improve the security situation in East Asia but created additional tensions.

    While Washington seeks to maintain its status as a regional hegemon, Beijing aims to gradually reduce the importance of the United States in the region. At best, both objectives and the policies derived from them can be partly contained, but they are not really compatible with each other. China's gain in power prompted many of its neighbours to call for a stronger, more balancing and more reassuring regional role of the United States. Since the confidence in the strength and reliability (*credibility*) of the USA as a guarantor of security declined already under Obama, some states such as Australia and Japan are looking for a complementary military commitment of the EU or important EU states as an additional *balancing* element. In the meantime, some actors (such as Japan) have instrumentalized the original *pivot to Asia* to also serve their own *assertiveness*. Nevertheless, most states in the region maintain close economic and political cooperation with the People's Republic. They are interested in both, cooperation with China *and* the USA, which fulfils an important prerequisite of a cooperative security policy.

5. Japan's contribution to the development of cooperative security in East Asia has been and is still limited. The short period of government of the Democratic Party (2009–12) did not lead to the urgently needed dissolution of internal impediments to reform and the originally sought redefinition of the Japanese role in the region, but to the return of the permanent Liberal Democratic Party rule in a decidedly right-wing conservative variant. The Abe government (2012–20) actively endeavoured to *normalise* foreign policy and to revise the constitution. With regard to World War II, Japan again openly pursues a policy of historical revisionism. As ever, its foreign policy remains heavily dependent on the USA. In the region, Japan is only accepted to a limited extent, mainly because of its problematic politics of the past. However, the rise of China and the threat perceptions associated with it have led to deep-rooted reservations about Japan being put aside, at least temporarily.

6. Western concepts for the Indo-Pacific region aim to position India as a counterweight to China. The foreign policy of the Indian Union is aimed at establishing the country as a comprehensive great power and as an in-

dependent pole in world politics (including the possession of nuclear weapons and a permanent seat on the UN Security Council). India's foreign policy traditionally follows the concept of *strategic autonomy*, which is accompanied by emphasising the principle of non-interference and rejecting alliance relations. Accordingly, India wants to avoid being instrumentalised by third parties and seeks to sustainably strengthen its own position in the Indo-Pacific region in the new constellation. The expansion of cooperation within the *Quad* group (Australia, India, Japan, USA) or the renewed partnership with the EU go hand in hand with the maintenance of relations with Russia, which have evolved over time. India has not changed this fundamental position even after Russia's attack on Ukraine. Under the Modi government, India is moving towards an increasingly authoritarian and Hindu nationalist rule, a development that is severely threatening or already has undermined the country's character as a pluralistic democracy. In view of these developments, the country can only to a limited extent be regarded as a *value partner* related to Western democracy.

7. Security cooperation in the Indo-Pacific region is characterised by institutional diversity and a shallow depth of content. Various institutions, as well as dialogue and cooperation formats (e.g., Asia-Pacific Economic Cooperation APEC, ASEAN Plus Three, East Asia Summit EAS), overlap not only with regard to their members, but also with regard to the tasks they are dealing with. The focus of these cooperation formats is on multilateral dialogue, while there is a lack of structures. At least as important as this multilateral cooperation are the bilateral alliance relations of the United States, e.g., with Japan, South Korea or (below alliance level) Taiwan. In spring 2021, the Biden administration initiated a stronger cooperation within the *Quad* format.

8. At present, the prospects for the development of cooperative security structures have to be viewed with scepticism:

   - The great powers USA, China, India and Japan are not (yet) interested in such steps. They are currently focusing on the priority of bilateral relations over multilateral cooperative security measures.
   - The smaller states do not hold enough influence to enforce their multilateral preferences on the agenda. This applies in particular to ASEAN, which used to play a major role in the development of security cooperation still in the 1990s.
   - The competition between the USA and China is increasingly becoming superimposed on the security constellation in East Asia and

the Indo-Pacific region and poses an additional complication to the making of regional arrangements.

9. Against this background, it seems necessary in terms of peace policy to follow a political line that does not fuel processes that cause enmity (and induce or activate emotions or stereotypes), counteracts *decoupling* and *containment*, clearly criticises China where necessary, but does not demonise it, and continues to maintain cooperation formats with China. The EU could pursue such a policy. A further securisation of all issues and relations in the Indo-Pacific region and an increasing dominance of the major conflict between the USA and China over the region's internal dynamics is likely to lead to a further consolidation and intensification of the conflict. Such a development is also likely to be reinforced by the EU or its leading powers when operating primarily as military actors (while at the same time neglecting the EU's actual advantages gained from its specialisation as a *normative power* and *broker*).

6 Recommendations for German and European Policies

"Europe must find its way in a world that is profoundly influenced by China in every dimension – not always in line with European conceptions, but also not fundamentally contrary to them. [...] With regard to its fundamental political orientation and the question of how to handle the ever-increasing conflict between China and the USA, Europe is facing an even more complicated challenge. The general principle to be followed should be to avoid being drawn into one of the camps and instead maintain constructive relations with both sides. Adopting the policy of 'strategic decoupling' recently pushed in Washington or even containing China serves neither European material interests nor the desire for a peaceful and open world that is not divided into camps. The fundamental normative dividing lines between Brussels and Beijing are apparent and will remain an element of rivalry. A policy of strategic autonomy and critical but not equal distance to both sides therefore offers the best chances of accommodating these differences. In this way, Europe can pursue an independent policy of détente and act as a mediator, bridging the gap of trust between the two superpowers. The political responsibility for peace strongly requires such a role to be fulfilled which is likely to be backed by strong support from numerous other states that also do not wish to return to a rigid bloc mentality." (Friedensgutachten 2021: 45, author's translation)

"In Southeast Asia, the EU is regarded as a desirable partner that is appreciated above all for its credible commitment to a rule-based and multilateral order. This could be used to establish Europe as a neutral, value-based power that exerts equal influence on all parties to the conflict. Europe's good reputation, however, also demands insistence on the recognition of international law and the acceptance of specific judgements to be expressed not only towards China but towards all parties to the conflict that have territorial claims. External actors such as the USA or Japan should also be reminded to reconsider their own claims for exclusive economic zones elsewhere." (Friedensgutachten 2021: 36, author's translation)

1. The European Union should not take sides in the major conflict between the USA and China, but adopt an independent position. Thus, it would live up to its goals of contributing to the shaping of the international order through its own initiatives, promoting peace and security and acting as an independent global actor. On many issues, the EU and the United States of America are able and likely to agree on common or similar positions that should also be asserted jointly. Unlike the USA, however, the EU does not see itself in a competition for global supremacy with China. It should also have no interest in promoting a new bipolarity as a structuring principle in a complex international system. The EU's strategy on China established in 2019 with its three elements of partnership, competition

and systemic rivalry provides a good framework for actively shaping the pattern of relations in all three dimensions.

The observations presented here on the common grounds for the co-operation between the EU and the USA apply to those administrations that are without doubt embedded in the democratic spectrum. There must be no such cooperation with a right-wing populist administration that includes right-wing extremists, if the EU wants to continue to consider itself a community of peace and values. The purpose and aim of the Atlantic Alliance (NATO) too are not above liberal democracy, but presuppose it.

2. The policy of great power competition between the USA, China and Russia, which was proclaimed by the Trump administration (2017) and is essentially continued by the Biden administration, has not been thought through. The objective of this long-term policy is not clearly defined. The implicit aim of fully implementing the USA's concepts of order and comprehensively asserting its hegemonic position in the international system seems questionable in view of structural trends towards multipolarity and the diffusion of power. The Biden administration has complemented the concept of fundamental competition with China by recognising the need for cooperation, i.e., on climate change or arms control. However, it has also extended this competition – and thus widened its boundaries even further – by an ideological dimension (*autocracy versus democracy*). The focus of the practical implementation is not on democracy but on containment and *rollback*. The proclamation of strategies that have no end point and no *exit* has a long but rather uninspiring tradition in the United States. A case in point is the *war on terror* proclaimed in 2001, whose preliminary results – up to the debacle in Afghanistan (2021) – can be assessed as moderately successful – or worse. The EU should stay away from strategies that do not have an end point, focus and exit. It should also be aware of the fact that these concepts do not include an independent role for it.

3. Human rights as the international order's third central pillar – together with the principles of sovereignty and the prohibition on the use of force – are not negotiable for Germany and the EU. According to the understanding of modern international law, the concept of human rights must not be limited to traditional civil liberties, but must also include social rights and participatory rights. The persistent advocacy of human rights is of great importance especially in the relations with non-Western states. While at no time did China and the EU have a common understanding on human rights in general, there are some areas where there used to be more

common ground than currently is. An EU human rights policy geared to actual progress should clearly identify deficits and favour a strategy of dialogue. Human rights and rule of law dialogues with the People's Republic of China should be continued and deepened. A country's credibility is invariably determined, to a great extent, by the implementation of human rights at home and the avoidance of double standards. Human rights problems must also be discussed with states like India or Singapore, which are still or have been until recently labelled as "partners with whom the West shares common values". It is evident from all past experience that, in the relationship between the EU or Germany and China, sanctions are an ambivalent instrument for achieving changes in behaviour. They are more likely to contribute to the hardening of political positions and make the sometimes- controversial dialogue more difficult. The EU should be aware of this when imposing sanctions in the event of human rights violations anyway.

4. The fact that international relations are increasingly governed by international law as a law of international cooperation is a great step forward in human history. For this reason alone, the progressing erosion of international law, especially by the actions of great powers, must not be accepted. This development contradicts the normative claim of the EU as a power that regards the *strength of law* as a central principle of the international order. Accordingly, the EU and Germany should strictly observe international law and clearly reject power-driven unilateral interpretations, breaches or double standards. With regard to territorial disputes in the Indo-Pacific region, this means that all EU member states should accept compulsory arbitration under the *UN Convention on the Law of the Seas*. They should also actively promote this objective in the region and the EU should also call on the United States of America to join and ratify this agreement.

5. Cooperation requires communication. Under the influence of the COVID-19 pandemic, the direct, politico-diplomatic, scientific or cultural exchange with China has decreased significantly over the past years. The strict *no-COVID* strategy and quarantine policy pursued by the People's Republic have also contributed to this development. It is in the interest of all parties involved to prevent a consolidation of this situation. In particular, scientific partnerships, relations and dialogue formats in areas such as climate change, health care or arms control should be restored, expanded and deepened gradually and as quickly as possible. Scientific exchange is a value in itself and can promote mutual understanding and cooperation.

6. The best strategy for economic competitiveness is to strengthen own innovation and technological leadership potentials by means of the EU. A targeted, long-term technology policy has a greater effect than protectionist measures or other steps aimed at reducing China's competitive advantages. Therefore, Germany and the EU should not participate in trade and technology wars waged to impede China's rise. The multilateral rules and the arbitral jurisdiction by the WTO constitute suitable bases for taking action against rule violations by China and other actors. As China's second-largest trading partner (next to ASEAN), the EU has considerable negotiating power which can be used to get closer to achieving the objectives of equal market access and comparable competitive conditions, i.e., reciprocity. Linking these issues to non-economic issues is not expedient.

7. The EU's Indo-Pacific Strategy (2021) and the relevant guidelines of the German Federal Government (2020 and 2023) follow the principle of inclusivity and endorse cooperative security and the strengthening of security relations in the Indo-Pacific region. The Federal Government in office until the end of 2021 only implemented this balanced approach partly, treating "cooperative security" as a task to be neglected and the "strengthening of security relations" as the actual task to be accomplished. There were no initiatives to support cooperative security structures or arms control. Only little more attention was paid to the development of relations with the large ASEAN community. Instead, military relations were strengthened with Australia and Japan – two states, which, like the United States, are pursuing a containment policy towards China that is rejected in the guidelines. Two-plus-two talks between foreign and defence ministers, a dialogue format unusual for German foreign policy, were agreed only with these states. While the Federal Foreign Office could not be seen to play a creative part, the Federal Ministry of Defence had de facto assumed the leading role. Remarkably enough, the strategic communication of the security policy guidelines for the Indo-Pacific was then left to the upper echelons of the German Navy. Unfortunately, the „traffic light coalition" – named after each of the coalition partners' colours – continued this approach; further neglecting cooperative security.

8. Partners sharing common values are not allies. *"Partnership of values"* refers to a partnership – defined with varying degrees of precision – based on certain common grounds; an *alliance partnership* usually also entails a contractually agreed obligation to provide assistance in the event of a conflict. Blurring these differences is a sign of ignorance with respect to security policy or a deliberately negligent handling of international law

categories, and this curtailed the freedom of action in Germany's foreign and security policy. Therefore, a return to legally sound concepts and accurate diplomatic language is required.

9. The EU and Germany do not play a decisive role in the conflict over Taiwan. They have no reasonable interest in aggravating or escalating the conflict. They want peace and stability in the Taiwan Strait. A war in East Asia would have wide-raging political and economic consequences that would by far exceed the impact of the Russian war of aggression against Ukraine.

   The EU and Germany should – primarily behind closed doors – try to persuade the US administration to clearly revert to the policy of *strategic ambiguity*, including the non-recognition of Taiwan's independence. To this end, diplomatic coordination or cooperation with the ASEAN states would also be useful.

   The EU and Germany should send a very clear signal to the People's Republic of China that a military attack on Taiwan would result in far-reaching sanctions by the EU that would come at high economic costs. They should also stick to their *One China policy* and clearly communicate this position – along with their call for de-escalation – in Beijing.

10. Following a decision by former Chancellor Konrad Adenauer, the Federal Republic of Germany has never had diplomatic relations with the Republic of China (Taiwan). It should continue to handle the development of relations with a high degree of conflict sensitivity. Strengthening the EU's and Germany's relations with Taiwan, for example in the economic and technological field, is possible. Status issues, however, should not be discussed or changed. Unilateral approaches by individual EU member states aimed at enhancing Taiwan's status do not contribute to the containment of the conflict. Germany should not support such isolated courses of action and communicate this clearly within the EU.

11. The potential for a security role of the EU and its member states in the Indo-Pacific region is rather low. This is mainly due to limited resources, limited common ground with regard to the development of a strategy, and already ongoing national, isolated approaches that predispose EU policy. In the Indo-Pacific region, too, the main specialisation advantages of the EU lie in its capabilities for balancing interests and promoting cooperative security. A build-up of military presences is in latent contradiction to this. With regard to the processes of cooperation and confrontation in the region, such a build-up stimulates the dynamics of confrontation without ultimately being able to influence this development. In addition, third

parties may successfully attempt to instrumentalise the EU and Germany for their goals.

These findings are confirmed by an analysis of the deployment of the German frigate *Bayern* to the Indo-Pacific region in 2021/22. Considered in isolation, the deployment of this ship is only an event of limited relevance. However, in the context of the accompanying rhetoric – non-inclusivity; "containment" of China; build-up of a larger national naval presence in the region; claiming to be sending a signal in support of a "rule-based international order" while at the same time working shoulder to shoulder with powers that endorse the merely selective acceptance of rules and values – it appears to be a highly problematic attempt to position Germany as a party to the conflict by means of strategic communication. Such a *framing* contradicts the policy guidelines for the Indo-Pacific region and is politically counterproductive. In addition, it does not contribute to a sustainable security policy.[6]

Germany should refrain from a permanent military presence in the region and instead strongly support – as part of an EU effort – ASEAN in particular, but also other like-minded states in their efforts for cooperative security and conflict settlement.

---

6 The „strategic communication" imparting the security policy components of the guidelines for the Indo-Pacific region, provided by the then Minister of Defence Kramp-Karrenbauer (2019–21), supported exactly this framing. At no time was the Minister interested in a dialogue with China. An analysis of public statements by Vice Admiral (retd.) Schönbach, Chief of the German Navy until his resignation on 22 January 2022, confirms this analytical finding and documents a worryingly limited level of knowledge about the greater Indo-Pacific region. Schönbach expressed his conviction that the rise of China could only be stopped by force: "This must end, and in the end, the only way to do this is to use force." Germany's military presence in the Indo-Pacific region would therefore have to be increased step by step. An alliance with Russia against China would be desirable (cf. Manohar Parrikar Institute 2022; Die Tageszeitung 2022).

Further Reading and References

Allison, Graham (2017): Destined for War: Can America and China Escape Thucy-dides's Trap?, New York.

Brands, Hal/Beckley, Michael (2022): Danger Zone. The Coming Conflict with China, New York.

Brunnermeier, Markus/Doshi, Rush/James, Harold (2018): Beijing's Bismarckian Ghosts: How Great Powers Compete Economically, in: Washington Quarterly, Volume 41, Issue 3, pp. 161–176.

Bundesregierung (2020): Policy guidelines for the Indo-Pacific: Germany – Europe – Asia: shaping the 21st century together), Berlin, available at: https://www. auswaertiges-amt.de/blob/2380500/331978a9d4f511942c241eb4602086c1/20090 1-indo-pazifik-leitlinien--1--data.pdf [last assessed on 25 August 2024].

Bundesregierung (2023): Strategy on China of the Federal Government of Germany, available at: https://www.auswaertiges-amt.de/blob/2608580/49d50fecc479304c3 da2e2079c55e106/china-strategie-en-data.pdf [last assessed 24 August 2024].

Cha, Victor D. (2023): Collective Resilience. Deterring China's Weaponization of Economic Interdependence, in: International Security, Volume 48. Issue 1, pp. 91–224.

Choong, William (2014): The Ties that Divide: History, Honour and Territory in Sino-Japanese Relations, Abingdon/New York.

Colby, Elbridge (2021): The Strategy of Denial. American Defense in an Age of Great Power Conflict, New Haven/London.

Cunningham, Fiona C. (2021): Cooperation under Asymmetry? The Future of US-China Nuclear Relations, in: Washington Quarterly, Vol. 44, Issue 2, pp. 159–180.

Deutscher Bundestag (2021): Regierungserklärung von Bundeskanzler Olaf Scholz (Government policy statement by Federal Chancellor Olaf Scholz), 15 December 2021, Stenographic Report, available at: https://dserver.bundestag.de/btp/20/200 08.pdf [last assessed on 3 January 2022].

European Union Chamber of Commerce in China/Mercator Institute for China Studies (2021): Decoupling: Severed Ties and Patchwork Globalisation, Berlin, available at: https://merics.org/sites/default/files/2021-01/Decoupling_EN.pdf [last assessed on 31 October 2022].

Fravel, M. Taylor (2019): Active Defense. China's Military Strategy since 1949, Princeton/Oxford.

Friedberg, Aaron L. (2011): A Contest for Supremacy. China, America, and the Struggle for Mastery in Asia, New York/London.

Friedensgutachten (2021): Europa kann mehr! Bonn International Conversion Center / Hessische Stiftung Friedens- und Konfliktforschung/Institut für Friedensfor-schung und Sicherheitspolitik (Hrsg.), Bielefeld. Online: http://friedensgutachten. de/user/pages/04.archiv/2021/02.ausgabe/FGA_2021_gesamt.pdf [last assessed on 31 October 2022].

Gareis, Sven B. (2020): Chinas Nuklearstrategie in einem neuen geopolitischen Umfeld. In: Ethik und Militär, Band 7, Nr. 1, S. 79–85.

Global Asia (2022): Taking Taiwan. The Risks, and Costs, of China Choosing Conflict. Band 17, Nr. 3, Seoul. Online: https://www.globalasia.org [last assessed on 31 October 2022].

Godehardt, Nadine (2020): Wie China Weltpolitik formt. Die Logik von Pekings Außenpolitik unter Xi Jinping, SWP-Studie, Berlin. Online: https://www.swp-berlin.org/publications/products/studien/2020S 19_China.pdf [last assessed on 31 October 2022].

Groten, David (2019): How Sentiment Matters in International Relations. China and the South China Sea Dispute, Opladen/Berlin/Toronto.

Hansel, Mischa/Harnisch, Sebastian/Godehardt, Nadine (Hrsg.) (2018): Chinesische Seidenstraßeninitiative und amerikanische Gewichtsverlagerung. Reaktionen aus Asien, Baden-Baden.

Harnisch, Sebastian (2016): China's international roles. Challenging or supporting international order? New York.

Hartmann, Wolf D./Maennig, Wolfgang/Wang, Run (2017): Chinas neue Seidenstraße. Kooperation statt Isolation – Der Rollentausch im Welthandel, Frankfurt am Main.

Heiduk, Felix/Wacker, Gudrun (2020): From Asia-Pacific to Indo-Pacific. Significance, Implementation and Challenges, SWP-Studie, Berlin. Online: https://www.swp-berlin.org/publikation/from-asia-pacific-to-indo-pacific [last assessed on 25 August 2024].

Hilpert, Hanns Günter/Sakaki, Alexandra/Wacker, Gudrun (2022): Dealing with Taiwan, SWP-Studie, Berlin. Online: https://www.swp-berlin.org/publikation/dealing-with-taiwan [last assessed on 25 August 2022].

Huang, Ying (2019): Die Chinapolitik der Bundesrepublik Deutschland nach der Wiedervereinigung. Ein Balanceakt zwischen Werten und Interessen, Wiesbaden.

Koalitionsvertrag zwischen SPD, Bündnis 90/Die Grünen und FDP (2021): Mehr Fortschritt wagen. Bündnis für Freiheit, Gerechtigkeit und Nachhaltigkeit, Berlin. Online: https://www.spd.de/fileadmin/Dokumente/Koalitionsvertrag/Koalitionsvertrag_2021-2025.pdf [last assessed on 12 February 2022].

Kreuzer, Peter (2014): Konfliktherd Südchinesisches Meer. HSFK-Report Nr. 2. Online: https://www.hsfk.de/fileadmin/HSFK/hsfk_downloads/report0214.pdf [last assessed on 14 November 2022].

Lewis, Jeffrey (2014): Paper Tigers. China's Nuclear Posture, Abingdon/New York.

Mair, Stefan (2022): Strategic Ties, Not Blocs. Why Germany Should Promote a Multipolar Order. In: 49security. Views on Germany's National Security Strategy. Online: https://fourninesecurity.de/en/2022/09/23/why-germany-should-promote-a-multipolar-order [last assessed on 31 October 2022].

Manohar Parrikar Institute for Defense Studies and Analyses (2022): Talk by Vice Admiral Kay Achim Schönbach, Chief of the German Navy, 21 January 2022. Online: https://www.youtube.com/watch?v=ODmkoGQwlTU&t=4049s [last assessed on 31 October 2022].

Mayer, Maximilian (2018): China's historical statecraft and the return of history. In: International Affairs, Band 94, Nr. 6, S. 1217–1235.

Mearsheimer, John J. (2001): The Tragedy of Great Power Politics, New York.

Meier, Oliver/Staack, Michael (2022): China's Role in Multilateral Arms Control. Online: https://www.fes.de/en/shaping-a-just-world/peace-and-security/article-in-peace-and-security/chinas-role-in-multilateral-arms-control [last assessed on 31 October 2022].

Miller, Chris (2022): Chip War. The Fight for the World's Most Critical Technology, London.

Mouritz, Frank (2021): The Influence of Economic Interdependence on US-China Relations. An Analysis of Economic Incentives for Continued Cooperation, Opladen/Berlin/Toronto.

Mühlhahn, Klaus (2021): Geschichte des Modernen China. Von der Qing-Dynastie bis zur Gegenwart, München.

Naß, Matthias (2021): Drachentanz. Chinas Aufstieg zur Weltmacht und was er für uns bedeutet, München.

Noesselt, Nele (2010): Alternative Weltordnungsmodelle? IB-Diskurse in China, Wiesbaden.

Noesselt, Nele (2020): China's New Silk Road Dreams. In: Berliner China-Hefte/Chinese History and Society, Band 52, Berlin.

Noesselt, Nele (2021): Chinese Politics. National and Global Dimensions, Baden-Baden.

Open Letter to the President and Congress on China Policy. In: The Washington Post, 4. Juli 2019. Online: https://www.openletteronuschina.info [last assessed on 30 May 2021].

Osterhammel, Jürgen (1989): China und die Weltgesellschaft. Vom 18. Jahrhundert bis in unsere Zeit, München.

Paul, Michael (2017): Kriegsgefahr im Pazifik? Die maritime Bedeutung der sino-amerikanischen Rivalität, Baden-Baden.

Presse- und Informationsamt der Bundesregierung (2014): Gemeinsame Erklärung zum Besuch von Staatspräsident Xi: Schaffung einer umfassenden strategischen Partnerschaft zwischen Deutschland und China. Press release 102, dated 28 May 2014. Online: https://www.bundesregierung.de/breg-de/suche/gemeinsame-erklae rung-zum-besuch-von-staatspraesident-xi-schaffung-einer-umfassenden-strategi schen-partnerschaft-zwischen-deutschland-und-china-411848 [last assessed on 30 May 2021].

Raine, Sarah/Le Miere, Christian (2013): Regional Disorder. The South China Sea Disputes, Abingdon/New York.

Rogelja, Igor/Tsimonis, Konstantinos (2020): Narrating the China Threat. Securitising Chinese Economic Presence in Europe. In: The Chinese Journal of International Politics, Band 13, Nr. 1, S. 103–133.

Rudd, Kevin (2022): The Avoidable War. The Dangers of a Catastrophic Conflict between the US and Xi Jinping's China, New York.

Rudolf, Peter (2019): The Sino-American World Conflict, SWP-Studie, Berlin. Online: https://www.swp-berlin.org/publikation/the-sino-american-world-conflict [last assessed on 25 August 2024].

Rudolf, Peter (2024): Konfrontationskurs. Der amerikanisch-chinesische Weltkonflikt, Freiburg/Basel/Wien.

Scherrer, Christoph (2021): America Second? Die USA, China und der Weltmarkt, Berlin.

Schmidt, Helmut (2004): Die Mächte der Zukunft. Gewinner und Verlierer in der Welt von morgen, München.

Schmidt, Helmut (2013): Ein letzter Besuch. Begegnungen mit der Weltmacht China, München.

Scobell, Andrew (2021): Constructing a U.S.-China Rivalry in the Indo-Pacific and Beyond, in: Journal of Contemporary China, Vol. 30, pp. 69–84.

Shambaugh, David (2013): China Goes Global. The Partial Power, Oxford.

Sommer, Theo (2019): China First. Die Welt auf dem Weg ins chinesische Jahrhundert, München.

Staack, Michael (Hrsg.) (2013): Asiens Aufstieg in der Weltpolitik, Opladen/Berlin/Toronto.

Staack, Michael/Groten, David (Hrsg.) (2018): China und Indien im regionalen und globalen Umfeld, Opladen/Berlin/Toronto.

Staack, Michael (2018): Strategische Partnerschaft zwischen China und Deutschland: Krisenfest und zukunftstauglich? In: Staack, Michael/Groten, David (Hrsg.) (2018): China und Indien im regionalen und globalen Umfeld, Opladen/Berlin/Toronto, S. 29–61.

Staack, Michael (2021): Mythos „China ist ein neues Reich des Bösen". In: Die Friedens-Warte, Vol. 94, Issue 3–4, S. 307–337.

Die Tageszeitung (2022): Flottenchef versenkt, 24 January 2022. Online: https://taz.de/Vizeadmiral-Kay-Achim-Schoenbach/!5829963 [last assessed 31 October 2022].

Tan, Nian/Su, Fei (2021): A New Estimate of China's Military Expenditure, SIPRI, Stockholm.

The Kremlin (2022): Joint Statement of the Russian Federation and the People's Republic of China on the International Relations Entering a New Era and the Global Sustainable Development, February 4, 2022. Online: http://en.kremlin.ru/supplement/5770 [last assessed 31 October 2022].

The White House (2003): President Bush Meets with President of China. Online: https://georgewbush-whitehouse.archives.goV/news/releases/2003/10/20031019-6.html [last assessed 31 October 2022].

The White House (2022): United States Strategic Approach to the People's Republic of China. Washington, D.C. Online: https://trumpwhitehouse.archives.gov/wp-content/uploads/2020/05/U.S.-Strategic-Approach-to-The-Peoples-Republic-of-China-Report-5.24vl.pdf [last assessed 31 October 2022].

The White House (2022): National Security Strategy. Washington, D.C. Online: https://www.whitehouse.gov/wp-content/uploads/2022/10/Biden-Harris-Administrations-National-Security-Strategy-10.2022.pdf [last assessed 31 October 2022].

Tong, Zhao (2024): The Real Motives for China's Nuclear Expansion. Beijing seeks Geopolitical Leverage More Than Military Advantage, in: Foreign Affairs, 3 May, 2024; https://www.foreignaffairs.com/china/real-motives-chinas-nuclear-expansion (last accessed 25 August 2024).

United Nations (1971): U.N. Resolution 2758, 25.10.1971. Online: https://web-archive-2017-ait.org.twun-res-2758-voted-to-admit-communist-china.html [last assessed 31 October 2022].

United States Department of State (2007): Press Conference of Secretary of State Condoleezza Rice. Online: https://2001-2009.state.gov/secretary/rm/2007/12/97 945.htm [last assessed 31 October 2022].

United States Department of State, Office of the Historian (1972): Joint Statement of the United States Following Discussions with Leaders of the People's Republic of China, Shanghai, 27.2.1972. Online: https://history.state.gov/historicaldocu ments/frus1969-76v17/d203 [last assessed 31 October 2022].

Van Alst, Niklas (2021): Die USA, Deutschland und der Fall Huawei. Zur Geopolitik und Geoökonomie des Internets, Opladen/Berlin/Toronto.

Vogel, Ezra F. (2011): Deng Xiaoping and the Transformation of China, Cambridge/ Massachusetts.

Weigelin-Schwiedzrik, Susanne (2023): China und die Neuordnung der Welt, Wien.

Winkler, Stephanie/Jerdén, Björn (2023): US foreign policy elites and the great reju-venation of the ideological China threat. The role of rhetoric and the ideologiza-tion of geopolitical threats, in: Journal of International Relations and Develop-ment, Vol. 26, pp. 159–184.

Wirth, Christian (2019): Whose „Freedom of Navigation"? Australia, China, the United States and the making of order in the "Indo-Pacific". In: The Pacific Re-view, Band 32, Nr. 4, S. 475–504.

Wirth, Christian (2022): How to Anchor Germany's Drifting Indo-Pacific Policy. GIGA Focus, Nr. 1, Hamburg. Online: https://www.giga-hamburg.de/en/publica tions/giga-focus/how-to-anchor-germanys-drifting-indo-pacific-policy [last as-sessed 31 October 2022].

Yuan, Xinyu (2020): Chinese Pathways to Peacebuilding, Geneva. Online: https:// repository.graduateinstitute.ch/record/298467 [last assessed 30 June 2021].

Zhao, Tingyang (2020): Alles unter dem Himmel. Vergangenheit und Zukunft der Weltordnung, Berlin.

Subject Index

The Author

Dr. Michael Staack, born in 1959, is Professor of International Relations at the Helmut Schmidt University/University of the German Armed Forces Hamburg since 2006 (Emeritus since 2024). From 1998 to 2001, he was the founding director of the Institute for German Studies in Minsk (Belarus) on behalf of the German Federal Government. Between 2001 and 2006, Michael Staack taught as professor at the University of the German Armed Forces in Munich. He was a research fellow at the Brookings Institution and the Georgetown University in Washington, D.C., and worked as a visiting professor at Beijing University, Beijing Foreign Affairs University and China Foreign Affairs University. From 2014 to 2017, he acted as advisor to the then foreign ministers of Germany and South Korea as a member of the High-level Advisory Group on the Foreign Policy Issues related to the re-unification of Korea. Professor Staack's main areas of work include Germany's foreign policy, security in East Asia and international governance on disarmament and arms control. Homepage: https://www.michael-staack.de/

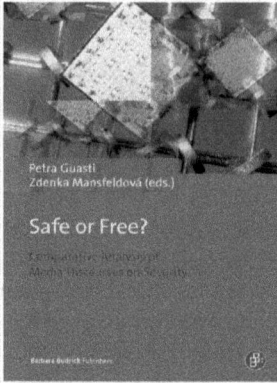

Petra Guasti
Zdenka Mansfeldová (eds.)

Safe or Free?

Comparative Analysis of
Media Discourses on Security

2025 • approx. 250 pp. • Pb. • approx. 33,00 € (D) • 34,00 € (A)
ISBN 978-3-8474-0684-6 • eISBN 978-3-8474-0853-6

One of the biggest dilemmas of our times is how much safety and security we desire and what price we are prepared to pay for it. By applying and advancing the methods of social research this book fills the gap in the study of security and security risks by analyzing unique data (media, survey, macro data) of transnational security issues in three areas of critical infrastructure – air transport, public transport and energy provision networks.

www.shop.budrich.de

GPSR Authorized Representative: Easy Access System Europe, Mustamäe tee
50, 10621 Tallinn, Estonia, gpsr.requests@easproject.com

www.ingramcontent.com/pod-product-compliance
Lightning Source LLC
Chambersburg PA
CBHW070032030426
42335CB00017B/2398